First

Respect

by Janet Riehecky

Consultant:
Madonna Murphy, PhD, Professor of Education
University of St. Francis, Joliet, Illinois
Author, *Character Education in America's Blue Ribbon Schools*

Capstone
press

Mankato, Minnesota

First Facts is published by Capstone Press,
151 Good Counsel Drive, P.O. Box 669, Mankato, Minnesota 56002.
www.capstonepress.com

Library of Congress Cataloging-in-Publication Data
Riehecky, Janet, 1953–
    Respect / by Janet Riehecky.
    p. cm.—(First facts. Everyday character education)
    Includes bibliographical references and index.
    ISBN 0-7368-3682-9 (hardcover)
    1. Respect—Juvenile literature. I. Title. II. Series: First facts. Everyday character education.
BJ1533.R4R54 2005
179'.9—dc22
                                                            2004018350

Summary: Introduces respect through examples of everyday situations where this character trait
    can be used.

Editorial Credits
Amanda Doering, editor; Molly Nei, set designer; Kia Adams, book designer; Kelly Garvin,
    photo researcher

Photo Credits
Brand X Pictures/Steve Allen, 20
Corbis/Bettmann, 16
Gem Photo Studio/Dan Delaney, cover, 1, 5, 6–7, 8, 9, 10–11, 12, 13, 19
Women's eNews/Debra DeBoise, 15

Capstone Press thanks Lee's Champion Taekwondo Academy and Master Colby Winkler for their
    help in photographing this book.

1 2 3 4 5 6 10 09 08 07 06 05

Table of Contents

Respect

Laura wants to play outside with a friend. Her mom is talking on the phone. Laura waits for her mom to finish talking before she asks to go outside. Laura shows respect by not **interrupting** her mom.

Fact!
Being respectful means treating everyone like they are important.

At Your School

Show respect at school. Respect people who are trying to study. Be quiet in the library.

Listening quietly to your teacher shows respect. Raise your hand if you want to speak.

With Your Friends

Respectful people are good friends. Treat your friends the way you want them to treat you. Respect their things. Be careful with your friends' toys.

Friends can still show respect when they disagree. Listen to your friends' **opinions**. Try to understand how they feel.

At Home

Be respectful of your family. Ask for **permission** before borrowing things from your sister.

Being polite shows respect to your family. Use good table manners. Say please and thank you.

> ## ! Fact!
> Knock on a closed door before entering. This shows that you respect your family members' privacy.

In Your Community

Respectful people are good citizens.
You can show respect by helping
people. Open the door for a person
in a wheelchair.

Respectful people know that everyone is important. Be respectful of people who are from a different **culture** than you.

Kenya Jordana James

At age 13, Kenya Jordana James started *Blackgirl* magazine. Kenya filled the magazine with information and stories for African-American girls. Kenya shows respect for her history and culture. She wants to help other girls be proud of who they are.

Korczak Ziolkowski

In 1939, Lakota Indian chiefs asked Korczak Ziolkowski to make a **statue** of Crazy Horse. Crazy Horse was a famous Lakota leader. Ziolkowski agreed to carve the statue out of mountains in South Dakota. Ziolkowski worked on the statue without pay. He carved the statue to show respect for the Lakota culture.

Fact!

Korczak Ziolkowski worked on the Crazy Horse statue for almost 36 years. He died in 1982. His family continues to work on the statue.

What Would You Do?

Laura has good news she wants to tell her friend. Laura wants to whisper to him while her teacher is talking. She knows it isn't respectful to talk while her teacher is talking. Still, she doesn't want to wait to share her news. What should Laura do?

Amazing but True!

Showing respect to the U.S. flag shows respect to the United States. The National Flag Code lists many ways to show respect to the U.S. flag. For example, the flag should never touch the ground.

Hands On: Write a Respect Letter

Who do you respect? Write a letter to someone who you feel is a good person.

What You Need

pen or pencil
paper
envelope

What You Do

1. Draw a line down the middle of the paper. On one side of the line, list people who you respect.
2. On the other side of the line, list why you respect those people. What good qualities do they have that make you respect them?
3. Choose one of the people on the list and write a letter to that person. Tell why you respect them. Thank him or her for being a good person.
4. Give the letter to that person. If you need to mail the letter, ask an adult to help you.

Glossary

culture (KUHL-chur)—a group of people's way of life, ideas, art, customs, and traditions

interrupt (in-tuh-RUHPT)—to start talking before someone else has finished talking

opinion (uh-PIN-yuhn)—the ideas and beliefs that a person has about something

permission (pur-MISH-uhn)—the okay to do something

statue (STACH-oo)—a model of a person or animal made from metal, stone, or wood

Read More

Kyle, Kathryn. *Respect.* Wonder Books. Chanhassen, Minn.: Child's World, 2003.

Loewen, Nancy. *Treat Me Right!: Kids Talk About Respect.* Kids Talk. Minneapolis: Picture Window Books, 2003.

Internet Sites

FactHound offers a safe, fun way to find Internet sites related to this book. All of the sites on FactHound have been researched by our staff.

Here's how:

1. Visit *www.facthound.com*
2. Type in this special code **0736836829** for age-appropriate sites. Or enter a search word related to this book for a more general search.
3. Click on the **Fetch It** button.

FactHound will fetch the best sites for you!

Index